A Toy Fights Bodhood

Jose V Futral

Certainly, banks are an essential component of our infrastructure—QED was the reason for the need for bailouts in 2008. What implications might the principle of reasonable returns have for them? Where is the right balance between responsibility and importance? When do fee increases begin to resemble price gouging? What qualifies as a secure and dependable service? Ultimately, what exactly are these enormous salaries and bonuses for? What value does society attach to the work that is supposed to be compensated?

Consider that the typical annual salary for a Ph.D. research scientist working on a cancer treatment is between $110,000 and $160,000. However, a banker who focuses on mergers and acquisitions is likely to make approximately $2 million; tens of millions from his CEO. Every year, top managers of hedge funds earn billions of dollars; Except for the rare occasions when they are brought to the attention of authorities for insider trading, their shadowy maneuvers are hidden from public view.33 Some would argue that bankers earn their money by taking risks. However, their self-description as fearless captains of industry is hardly credible if they are putting other people's money at risk using black box methods with no personal risk. Similar to how infl ated grade-curves in schools create inflationary expectations throughout the economy, such enormous takes When their friends in government are so much wealthier, how can health reformers demand that surgeons accept lower pay? The bounty paid to the bankers causes values to fluctuate and decline.

For their essential services, banks charge a hefty price. Take into consideration the credit card late fee; The bank had already taken a cut of every purchase you made, even before you had to pay it. Take into consideration the enigmatic fees eating away at your 401(k) and the costs associated with transactions whenever your broker buys or sells. The churning of fees significantly affects the livelihoods of financial professionals. However, how much of a value do these professionals actually add to the business?

It would appear that not much. The 2008 financial crisis is only the most recent illustration of how quick "scores" of financial intermediaries deplete Main Street investors' resources. According to Wallace Turbeville, a former investment banker, the United States' "excessive wealth transfer to the financial sector" amounts to $635 billion annually. Leading London bankers, according to a New Economics Foundation (NEF) study, "destroy £7 of social value for every pound in value they generate."34 35 According to the Kauffman Foundation, an "ever-expanding financial sector is depleting the talent pool of potential high-growth company founders." "Whatever one's opinion of their methods may be, Turbeville, NEF, and

Kauffman are at least asking difficult and necessary questions about how the world of finance interacts with the real economy. Why go to the trouble of developing a new product or service when you can take on much less risk and net more money as a financier rating and juggling investments?"37 Researcher Thomas Philippon believes that finance firms are becoming more expensive even though they pride themselves on forcing managers in other industries to cut costs and reduce wages.40 Macroeconomists J. Bradford DeLong and Stephen Cohen calculate that the United States experienced a 7% drop in manufacturing concurrently with a 7% expansion in financial transactions. This would be the first step toward a realistic assessment of value in the financial sector.38 It would be a sobering exercise.39 Researcher Thomas Philippon believes that finance firms are becoming This means, for instance, that Wall Street has pressured pharmaceutical firms to lay off thousands of drug developers and cut R&D in favor of "core competencies," punishing Merck for investing in research and rewarding Pfizer for cutting it.41 This means, for example, that Wall Street has pressured pharmaceutical firms to lay off thousands of drug developers and cut R&D in favor of "core competencies." Each reduction in scientific investment may appear rational at the time, but the long-term effects are chilling—both medically for all of us and environmentally for the millions of Americans who are exiled from sectors that are relatively prosperous into low-paying service jobs, or worse. Is it any wonder that people on the outside feel like they are fighting over smaller pieces of the same pie? 43 This is a zero-sum game in which the goal is not sustainable investment or the construction of lasting value, but rather complex risk-shifting that mulcts the unwary. 42 The financial sector is currently more invested in positional competition for buying power than in increasing the number of goods and services available for purchase. If its leading examples weren't so utterly dependent on public assistance to stay afloat, the self-seeking might be excused. We ought to anticipate significantly more in terms of public service from these critical financial institutions in light of their too-big-to-fail status.

Making, Taking, and Faking: The great illusion of contemporary governance is that endlessly making claims to future wealth will somehow result in a more productive economy44. A similar illusion is beginning to permeate the search and reputation industries.

Setting up bidding wars—for a chance to finance an investment, to appear in front of an audience, or to qualify for an opportunity—is one way intermediaries can become wealthy without increasing the total number of goods and services produced. There is a good reason why these organizations put in so much effort to conceal their methods: When the curtain is drawn, the economic wizards appear to be nothing more than contest organizers in which they would never be able to participate. They are referees, not players.

The millions of creators whose work is being so lucratively rated, searched, and shuffled are herded into global labor markets that are becoming increasingly competitive. We say that we value "makers" over "takers" and "fakers," and if the reputation, search, and finance sectors are left to their own devices, they will continue to siphon effort away from productive innovation and into more shuffle and scrambling.45 But if we want to identify who is who, we need a society that can be understood. Due to shady deals between content owners and intermediaries, internet companies are not assisting us in achieving that objective. Perfect online control schemes would grant copyright holders too much control, trampling free speech and a thriving remix culture on their way to that singular goal. In secret, slowing down or downranking pirate sites does little to solve the underlying problems of the content industries—or the individuals they (used to) provide income to.46 However, compensation can come in many different forms. In the past, Congress imposed a small fee per copy—a practice known as compulsory licensing—when it realized that new technology would lead to widespread copying.47 The recording industry itself has repeatedly (and successfully) lobbied to force composers and lyricists to accept a government-set compulsory license. This system, which is still in place for many works, separates control (over their use) from compensation (for works).

In the wild west of unrestricted Internet distribution, according to some, the compulsory licensing system cannot function. However, in Promises to Keep, Harvard law professor William W. Fisher makes a comprehensive and persuasive proposal: Law, technology, and entertainment's future The technology that leads to its unpaid duplication would be taxed lightly under the Fisher plan, which would help support culture. The government could also levy such fees on search engines and carriers and distribute them to creatives48. Fisher wants artists to be paid based on how often people actually watch or listen to their work;

Dean Baker has called for "artistic freedom vouchers," which would let taxpayers choose who they want to give money to each year ex ante. The current maze of copyright laws and chaotic, secret downrankings are likely to be less effective than either strategy. Fisher estimated in 2004 that a broadband subscriber fee of $6 per month would cover all of the music and movie industry revenue that was allegedly lost due to piracy.49 However, given the extreme and rising level of electronic inequality, such fees will need to be limited and, hopefully, progressively linked to income and wealth. They might be collected most effectively as a user fee with a sliding scale. Similar to the tax that was imposed to help fund the Affordable Care Act, a modest tax on wealthy homeowners' unearned investment income would also be beneficial in this situation. Culture has beneficial externalities, just like health care does. Unfortunately, the Recording Industry Association of America and the Motion Picture Association of America appear to be about as enthusiastic for a public option in entertainment as private insurers have been about it in health care.50 It deserves more support from those who are best able to pay for society's common needs. Because of this opposition, some people might dismiss Fisher's idea as a pipe dream. After all, our political system could not handle anything even remotely resembling a new tax.51 But what is the alternative? The Stop Online Piracy Act (SOPA), which would deny due process to alleged infringers, threaten free expression, and grant sweeping, unprecedented powers to copyright and trademark owners, was the content industry's leading legislative initiative in 2012. SOPA, like fusion centers, would accelerate government-industry surveillance through an unreliable partnership. What does it say about our Congress that it is more willing to amplify a police state that is dominated by oligopolists in the content industry than it is to revise and broaden an enduring licensing system that helps struggling journalists, artists, and musicians? The problem of piracy will dramatically decrease if content is made affordable and accessible.52 Contemporary politics in the United States has prioritized policing and punishment while marginalizing the welfare state and its support for the arts and commons. We should not be surprised if the political economy of intellectual property enforcement shifts to vertically integrated firms that use control over bottlenecks to monitor, deter, and perhaps ultimately ban content that threatens professions.53 Black box interventions by carriers and search engines merely take this punitive impulse into the private sector, where it is unbalanced by the usual reporting requirements and appellate checks on law enforcement abuses. After inspiring a large group of internet users to 204 THE BLACK BOX SOCIETY support the fundamental principles of due process, free speech, and online accountability, SOPA was ultimately repealed. But this conflict was just the beginning of a much more contentious discussion about how digital revenues should be distributed.

Conflicts between creatives and intermediaries, like those between providers and insurers in health care, will have a significant impact on our daily lives.

We should also be open to skepticism regarding technocratic solutions55 because Fisher's proposals would rely on pervasive surveillance of what is being listened to and watched in order to work well. Stopping SOPA is only one small step toward preserving a fair, free, and democratic culture online.

They will encourage extensive gaming if they are solely based on "number of downloads" or "number of views." Artists who allegedly manipulated their view count (either to increase ad revenue or appear more popular than they actually are) have already been the subject of scandals on YouTube. That gaming will, in turn, lead to countermeasures, which keep track of who is watching and liking what. Do we really need a central authority to gather all of this data just to make sure Lady Gaga earns, say, fifty times more money than the Magnetic Fields?

It is possible that allocating revenue from the entertainment industry in this manner amounts to "modulation," which is an effort to monitor and exercise soft control over particular communities (in this case, artists).56 We ought to reevaluate the plasticity of institutions like mandatory license fees.

In order to provide all artists with some degree of security, perhaps a minimum compensation should be established (WPA 2.0?). and maximum gains, in order to discourage high-end gaming. It's possible that the endeavor to precisely match reward to "value," as measured by the number of times something is viewed or watched, does not succeed in terms of economics: A particularly successful business may complete its "work" in one sitting. Or, a person might value one experience of a particularly moving song over 100 background music plays.

The larger point is that there is not just a conflict between the copyright maximalism of dominant industry players and the play of creativity. Even the most progressive reform ideas have the potential to unintentionally alter creative endeavors in some way. These considerations have frequently been blocked by the legal establishment: We'll worry about the law and money, and we'll let the artists figure out the creative side themselves."

But the experience of play and creativity are at the heart of the business, and they shouldn't be treated as "add-ons" or in the background of legal discussions. If we don't take into account which forms of artistic creation are better and worse from the perspective of the creators themselves, we won't be able to develop sound cultural policy.

What if it turns out that law is nearly incapable of accurately balancing risk and reward? John Kay's insights from Obliquity come to mind: Why It Is Best to

Reach Our Objectives Indirectly, and in this spirit, I'll make a side note to illustrate my point.

At least in my experience, the wealth of a spouse or family member is the best indicator of whether a person will work in the arts or start their own business. The message is out: It is simply too risky to attempt to earn a living as a painter, musician, actor, or poet, especially in light of the ongoing pressure to reduce Medicaid, food stamps, and welfare benefits in the United States.

However, the possibility of failure has not been as chilling in other nations, where the social safety net has been more generous.

Take for instance J. K. Rowling's fate, who, in her own words, hit "rock bottom" while writing and was forced to rely on the welfare system in Britain. She was able to establish herself in the literary industry after receiving support for a few years; without it, Harry Potter might not have been written. One bright spot for the marginally employed in the

United States is the Affordable Care Act's 2014 implementation.

Perhaps in decades to come, we will discover that the guarantee of health insurance policies through state exchanges and subsidies to purchase them was the primary impetus for artistic careers and employment of all kinds. By providing some breathing room for the inevitable slew of creative industry failures, health policy experts might be able to contribute more to creativity than all copyright policymakers put together.

I am aware that this strategy will be opposed by the tired rhetorical dichotomy between socialism's evils and traditional American capitalism. But which is more statist, a universal basic income that significantly reduces the need to deploy either a or b, a system for all-seeing Google, YouTube, and Facebook check-ins to report on what you're watching, or DHS contractors busting down the doors of copyright infringers? As the interpenetration of state and business in government and law enforcement serves an ever-shrinking set of interests, the specter of socialism becomes an ever-more laughable distraction.

On the Narrowing Gap Between Business and Government The "free markets vs. state" debates that permeate public discourse in the United States refer to a duality that is becoming more apparent rather than real. Think about health care. That "market" is rife with state-mandated licensing and quality regulations on the one hand.

On the other hand, private contractors are used by government programs like Medicare to determine eligibility, provide benefits, and profit from those benefits. Patterns in finance are similar. The Chicago Board of Trade, which is essentially a "market" institution, can only operate within a set of guidelines. We all know that market orders are influenced by political decisions, which are influenced by the market in turn as the beneficiaries of past political decisions use moneys gained in commerce to further future political ends.59 For example: Google's corporate lobbying spend was second only to that of General Electric in 2012.58 U.S. financial institutions quickly turned to the government (the president, Congress, and Federal Reserve) when mortgage-backed securities began to fail after years of exploiting subprime borrowers. These institutions also moved quickly to protect their prestige. However, ordinary borrowers did not receive the same level of protection from the government. According to the protesters' remark, "Banks got bailed out, we got sold out." Large financial institutions then employed countless lobbyists to weaken the Dodd-Frank Act and its subsequent implementation, leveraging their financial windfall into future political advantages.

In addition, key officials quickly characterized elite panic over financial markets—in this instance, the failure of overleveraged financial institutions—as an understandable and appropriate response to a fatal threat to the economy. The Kafkaesque Home Affordable Modification Program

(HAMP)—an intervention as sluggish and feckless as its clunky name suggests—was met with the desperation of typical borrowers.

Since industry has more power over its regulators than the regulators have over industry, many people refer to this influence as "capture." However, the term "capture" is too static to describe the actual situation.

An equally inert SEC or Fed cannot control a stable "Wall Street." Instead, certain segments of the industry masterfully outmaneuver rivals, gain agency influence, and alter their plans. Some businesses benefit from the new regulatory environment, while others suffer. The businesses boosted by the new order now have even more cash available to influence subsequent orders. An agency or industry can be driven far from its original set of values, goals, and strategies by those adept at shuffle-boarding between Washington, New York, and (now) Silicon Valley.

Charles E. Lindblom, a Yale social scientist, proposed a better term than "capture" for this mutual influence and transformation:

"circularity. "60 As we enter the information age, the revolving door between the dominant business sectors and the government is clearly increasing, which has unsettling implications. The rules of our black box society have been established by people, not some nameless abstraction like "industry."61 The stakes are too high for us to ignore this new reality: that politicians and bureaucrats will only go so far as to harm the business community's interests. The American state, which has been taming monopolization since at least the Sherman Act of 1890, is now more likely to promote the biggest winners in the economy than to ensure a level playing field for future competition. In addition, the search, reputation, and intelligence sectors' black box technologies can now be supported by the state's immense powers of compulsion and enforcement. Pundits indulge in a naive fixation on the outmoded polarity between "state" and "market" solutions, ignoring actual threats. This only leads to more misery and paralysis; It is a guarantee that we will never attain the societal ideals of security, fairness, and dignity that the majority of us aspire to, if not in exactly the same way. It's time to reevaluate where we want to go next and what stands in our way.

208 THE BLACK BOX SOCIETY The Promise of Public Alternatives The government regulates not only to promote private wealth, but also because industry performs some essentially public functions alongside its private profi t-seeking ones. As a result, government regulation is necessary. We might begin to see some real accountability if we, as citizens, directly

promoted those public functions.

We know from experience that open-source software can function as well as—sometimes better than—proprietary algorithms, and there is no reason why this shouldn't be true of a public scoring system. For instance, the government might commission a public credit scoring system and test its predictive power against closed, proprietary scores62. Public credit reporting systems are used in other countries.64 If the idea of transparent evaluative standards succeeds in consumer finance, it might come to play a larger role in reputational software in general. Once it got up to speed, financial regulators could require some lenders to use the transparent system or arrange lot programs for its partial deployment.63 Public credit reporting systems are used in other countries.64 In addition, compared to a system that is only understood, valued, and monitored by a few, a system that is fully open to the scrutiny of thousands of experts who are invested in its success may see its errors and omissions detected and fixed more quickly (and fairly).

Another option is to use public Internet facilities. Google is now taking on the more public role of scanning, indexing, and archiving books that aren't (individually) commercially viable, and Amazon is getting close to the status of a book duopolist. The Library of Congress (LOC) is located where? According to cultural theorist Siva Vaidhyanathan, a private company "step[ped] into a vacuum created by incompetent or gutted public institutions" in Google Book Search. Vaidhyanathan attributes its very existence to a "public failure." 65 A public book search program could use a content base from an LOC archive. Similarly as Government medical care offers benchmarks for inclusion choices and for private back up plans' installment rates (and gives admittance to want to those not served

by confidential protection showcases), a public book

search might both supplement at any point Google Books and help those not served by it.66 It would

or on the other hand ga nize the huge computerized data set in a straightforward manner, permitting us

TOWARD AN Understandable SOCIETY 209

no less than one book proposal framework that is both understandable and exhaustive.

At the moment, we don't really know how systems like Amazon's or Google's recommend books on topics like "obesity" (do you first see books that promote or criticize diet pills?) or "conflict in Palestine," "regulation of banks," or "Google's antitrust issues" Some opportunities for library scientists to apply ancient theories and principles to current ranking and filtering issues would come from a public ordering. If it had access to the data that underpins Google's and Amazon's dominance, a non-profit organization like the Digital Public Library of America

Foundation might also be able to offer a different point of view.

The issues in finance necessitate a more in-depth response because they are deeper than those in the reputation and search industries. In exchange for its implicit and explicit subsidies, the government ought to establish a more equitable reciprocity with the financial sector by demanding control. The health care industry has once again led the way. Major hospitals, like major financial institutions, are supported by the government. Subsidies come in a variety of forms under the Medicare and Medicaid systems. However, hospital participation in those systems is contingent on their compliance with stringent audits, emergency care provision, and quality standards. Health regulators regularly accomplish far more than financial regulators ever do.

This need not be the case. Congress could require agencies like the Securities and Exchange

Commission and the Commodity Futures Trading Commission to create incentives for straightforward and socially valuable investment. The Federal Reserve could limit the use of its low-interest "discount window" to banks that allocate capital in ways that improve productivity, rebuild infrastructure, reduce inequality, and recognize the value of all labor.67 A tax on financial transactions would also discourage the complicated trading schemes that are hidden behind some black box financial products and the volatility they cause.

In addition, the government could follow in the footsteps of the (spontaneous) social movement to "Move Your Money" out of the big banks and encourage citizens to reward transparency and penalize excessive complexity. It could make it possible for post offices to offer banking services, giving the millions of Americans who are "unbanked" 210 THE BLACK BOX SOCIETY a useful low-cost option.68 This is not a radical idea: For nearly a century, the Bank of North Dakota has provided loans to the state's farms and businesses.69 Public banking may also provide incentives for investments in the social good. Pension plans could also place an emphasis on old-fashioned "value investing," with specific commitments to understandable business plans70. Although staunch laissez-faire advocates denigrate socially responsible investing as a form of European socialism, such ideas have a long history in the United States. Rexford Tugwell wanted a commission to "encourage or discourage the flow of capital into various industries."71 Financial reform planners during Franklin Roosevelt's administration envisioned agencies that would "direct the flow of new investment in private industry" toward socially beneficial projects and away from the kind of self-dealing that was prevalent during the Roaring Twenties (and the more recent housing bubble). "72 Given the shameful state of America's roads, bridges, and public transportation today, would it be excessive to ask the Fed to purchase "infrastructure bonds" to supplement its vast holdings of mortgage-backed securities?73 FDR's advisors also took a direct approach to financial stability; Adolf Berle, a specialist in corporate governance, suggested that a company "exercise a real control over undue expansion of groups of credit instruments." "74 His proposal is just as relevant now as it was then.75 The dynamic of circularity teaches us that regulators and regulated cannot reach a stable, static equilibrium.

Many of the black box dynamics we saw unleashed in finance arose out of failed attempts to fudge this tension, such as the credit agencies' role as a "soft" regulator or the government's wink-wink, nod-nod (non)assurances regarding its backing of Fannie and Freddie and large financial institutions.77 That pattern continues to this day: According to Richard Fisher, president of the Federal Reserve Bank of Dallas, it is almost certain that the government will bail out a massive financial institution if too many of its bets go TOWARDS AN INTELLIGIBLE SOCIETY 211 bad.78 Credit ratings reflect the same assumption: the authors of Dodd-Frank claim that their bill addresses the issue of companies that are too large to fail. The risks posed by megabanks are too complex to quantify, but the smart money is betting that the government will intervene when they are in danger.

After the crisis, experts in finance have been fixated on structure issues: For instance, how can we guarantee that banks are smaller, less interconnected, and have better capital to lower the risk of failure and its repercussions? However, substance-based questions are much more crucial to constructing a resilient society. For instance, where ought to the incorrectly invested capital in the MBS/CDO/CDS hall of mirrors have been distributed? From basic research and education to infrastructure and antibiotics, Mariana Mazzucato, Geoff Mulgan, Joseph Stiglitz, and Robert Kuttner have all provided compelling responses. We must pay attention to their work. "Leaving it to the fi nance experts" is a recipe for decline because the success of the financial industry bears no inevitable relationship to the long-term health of the economy. As a result, all we can reliably anticipate in the future is that capital will be allocated to whatever instruments lead to the highest fees for self-serving intermediaries.79 Finance can be extractive or uplifting, narrowly short-termist or focused on the needs of society as a whole in terms of infrastructure and investment. We need a government that is interested in forward-thinking industrial policy and willing to enforce its interest in order to consistently address those needs80. This attitude is currently lacking in Washington. However, the government has the potential to use its hold on the budget to its advantage in the past. The Chinese investment in green technology, rare earths, education, and infrastructure ought to be America's Sputnik moment. Again, bienpensant economists will find these proposals to be excessively statist, but take into consideration the alternatives. It is time to allocate more of our resources to businesses that are likely to yield real and fairly distributed returns.81 Our government sector's law enforcement system has clearly failed to deter or properly punish illegal behavior. Similar to Terry Fisher's proposal for Internet content, mass surveillance is required, as described in the preceding chapter, to fully enforce information advantage in the industry. I borrowed this model from the health care industry, where a horde of contractors examines billing records to spot fraud and abuse. Paying physicians salaries rather than "per-procedure" is one alternative health care model that is intended to prevent overbilling and overtreatment. Imagine if this method were to take the place of Wall Street's bonus culture, where the annual pay of the majority of key players pales in comparison to the bounty offered during a banner year of spectacularly successful risks. Sure, there are concerns that salary-based pay will encourage shirking in the health care industry. Restoring Trust For far too long, we have assumed that the primary objective of financial regulation is disclosure.83 We like to believe that when every investor has the same key data about a security as its seller, the financial playing field will eventually be leveled. However, given how destructive financial innovation has been over the past decade, perhaps bankers ought to work less, at least until they can better demonstrate how their sector contributes to real productivity.82 Restoring Trust Additionally, sunlight is sometimes the "best disinfectant." "84 However, not always. Truth" is all too frequently told in a slant. Additionally, trust is erroneous when that takes place too frequently.

Recently, trust issues have begun to afflict not only the financial sector but also the most prominent search and reputation providers. The "rocket scientists" who were adored by the media before the crisis have lost some of their luster.85 The giants of Silicon Valley are now appearing more like "Wall Street West," groups motivated by lust for quick money. In terms of the financial industry as a whole, it is still rife with scandal, the Libor rigging mess being the most recent example.

Each of its issues can be explained as the result of a few bad apples; They all point to widespread rot. Bankers and executives in Silicon Valley alike are tempted by the prospect of making easy money by merely manipulating large volumes of transactions. Transparency and openness can be trampled upon by a culture of speed, scale, and speculation.

In his memoir Bailout, former prosecutor Neil Barofsky put it best: "The incentives are to cheat, and cheating is profitable because there are no consequences." "86 To those in charge of a bank with TOWARD AN INTELLIGIBLE SOCIETY 213 more than $50 billion in revenue, even a $450 million fraud is about as irritating as a mosquito bite.87 Penalties in Silicon Valley are an order of magnitude less severe. Even though Google made $22.5 million in just four hours, the FTC said that was a new record. Facebook paid $10 million to settle one case.88 The FCC once "punished" Google with a $25,000 fine. We owe a lot of this to black boxes, as it is a broken enforcement model. What they cannot comprehend cannot cause outrage. Furthermore, there are no repercussions for the politicians who are ultimately to blame unless there is public concern about the insignificant severity of the penalties for breaking the law.

Black Boxes' Limitations: A Hayekian Perspective It's true that black boxes make things easier; They speed up and save money on everyday transactions. The changes I propose would cause delays. They would spend money that would probably end up going to us. They would also consume time. A copyright complaint is dealt with within milliseconds by an automatic algorithm; People would take longer to evaluate a website's claim of fair use than that. To determine when negative credit information is less trustworthy than the person it is praising, credit raters would need to use human judgment and time.

I am certain that think tanks will make dire predictions regarding the costs of such initiatives. It is easy to predict the loss of tens of thousands of jobs if financial transactions are taxed or if credit bureaus are required to provide a full and fair accounting of their actions. However, whether they will be as forthcoming with the identity of their sponsors remains to be seen.)89 These kinds of studies have been purchased by Wall Street firms on multiple occasions and promoted in lobbying campaigns. However, as law professor John C. Coates has demonstrated, cost-benefit analysis of regulation can be yet another application of natural science methods to social science predictions.90 Despite industry predictions of doom, it is equally plausible that accountability in the reputation, search, and finance sectors would create jobs rather than eliminate them. Accountability necessitates human judgment, and only humans are capable of ensuring that domination and discrimination are not encoded invisibly into our social relations as they become increasingly automated.

214 THE BLACK BOX SOCIETY Another factor that contributes to the excessive efficacy of black boxes is the fact that information does not always permit generalization. For instance, the homogenizing effects of national underwriting standards on local housing markets are harshly criticized by Tufts University professor Amar Bhidé, who has experience in both finance and consulting. Hayek's fundamental insight was that

nobody knows everything about how goods and services in an economy should be priced, and that no one central decision maker can ever really grasp the idiosyncratic preferences, values, and purchasing power of millions of individuals.92 That kind of knowledge, Hayek said, is distributed. He criticizes black boxes from a Hayekian perspective, exposing our giant finance firms for having flaws that are eerily reminiscent of Communist central planners.91

Today, Hayek's most ardent supporters tend to believe that he was only expressing criticism of the government. However, the financial sector is highly concentrated and linked to state power. According to Bhidé, its centralization is also troubling and should be replaced by more localized decision-making. For instance, a loan officer in Phoenix would be much more likely than a high-level manager several hundred miles away to identify questionable local mortgage applicants. A Hayekian critic of black box firms could take this line of reasoning even further because a local bank putting its own money on the line (originating loans to keep them) would have a strong incentive to clearly estimate the potential risks and rewards of its decisions.93 Why should Google control such a large portion of the Internet? Isn't its rapid acquisition of start-ups a Promethean plan to consolidate more computing talent into a single organization? The same could be said for Apple's hold on its app empire or even

Facebook's dominance of social networking.94 A committed Hayekian could easily argue for far more aggressive antitrust enforcement in the tech industries.95 Black Box Endgame The reputation, search, and finance industries have formed powerful alliances due to their shared values, procedures, and (increasingly) cultures. The first two are based on data, whereas Wall Street securities TOWARDS AN INTELLIGIBLE SOCIETY 215 appear to be more tangible. However, while the differences are real, they are not as fundamental as the similarities. In the end, they are all in the information industry. Money, along with all of its derivatives, is nothing more than information about the quantity of our collective goods and services that it can demand. In addition, reputation and search firms are establishing new currencies for allocating attention and opportunity. Each of these businesses tries to gather information in order to make quick gains. However, we should never lose sight of the fact that the numbers displayed on their computers have real consequences, determining who receives funding and is located and who is discredited or omitted.

All rely on secrecy to safeguard the quick scores-related information. However, a number of different forms of secrecy could have been the subject of this book. Why not compare and contrast Wall Street and Silicon Valley? Important principles like dignity, fairness, and privacy are gravely in jeopardy thanks to the leading Internet and finance firms. Too frequently, self-protective black box practices and irrelevant distractions obscure this threat, which is increasingly intertwined with the power of the government. Over the past few decades, the political debate in the United States has boiled down to arguments about "market forces" or "state provision." In the meantime, the nimble businessmen behind reputation, search, and finance firms exploit (and create) issues that neither the market nor the state can resolve on their own.

They see the tug-of-war between the market and the state as a pas de deux, and the black box society's core is the blurring of this conventional distinction. The majority of this book's "markets" are markets for information regarding an individual's likelihood of clicking on an advertisement. pay for medical care; repay a loan. This kind of information is valuable only if it is exclusive, and only if the entire state's power can be used against anyone who discloses it without permission.

C. Wright Mills, a sociologist, wrote a 1956 sketch of the American "power elite": the government, the military, and the corporations. Mills saw these entities in their Cold War context in rough equipoise, each with its own distinct base of power (the ability to force others to do things they wouldn't normally do). Over the course of the twentieth century, Mills' division has become less and less relevant; For instance, the military's domestic power dwindled after the fall of the Berlin Wall, and 9/11 brought about the revival of a defense, intelligence, and policing complex. However, his idea continues to pique people's interest.96 Some social theorists have modified Mills' typology to account for the rise of other significant actors like the media. However, if Mills' "triangle of power" needs to be updated, its quaintness stems more from its members' separate but equal status than from the fact that it did not include other power centers.

Public servants are constantly tempted to "cash out" for private sector pay because of the revolving door dynamics of the twenty-first century. As a result, they are unwilling to do anything that could disrupt either their own main opportunity or similar opportunities for their peers and protégés.

We must recognize the new landscape if we are to free our political process from its antiquated and self-serving rut. Instead of assuming that the state should simply get out of the way of markets, this requires directly studying the "ideal role of the state in the economic and social or gani za tion of a country."97 This is the task of the classic social science of political economy, a method that integrates long-diverse fields. With this information, we can resume the crucial discussion that has been stalled for so long: What kind of society do we truly desire?

Toward an Intelligible Society Capitalist democracies increasingly employ automated risk and opportunity allocation strategies. Some of the most dynamic, significant, and significant players in the information economy are the businesses that own these processes. In order to organize vast amounts of data, each of these vices makes use of secret algorithms. The technology's ancient goal of forecasting the future with a modern twist of statistical sobriety is obvious.

However, in an atmosphere of secrecy, inaccurate or even disastrous predictions are just as likely to be made as good ones.

As a result, despite how beneficial it may be to the insiders who manage it, the widespread application of black box modeling poses a threat to society as a whole. It's bad enough when inaccuracies that innocent people can't dispute and may not even be aware of cause harm or label them as security threats, gold thieves, or credit risks. The power of algorithms combined with unfair or inappropriate considerations results in the failures they purport to merely predict, making modeling even worse.

Furthermore, algorithmic control fails on its own terms when errors are sufficiently systematic. That took place most egregiously during the 2008 financial crisis. Only hundreds of billions of dollars from the government were used to restore order, and even during this enormous intervention, secrecy prevailed; At the time, many of the involved banks' identities were kept secret.

Today's educated citizenship necessitates more than just a comprehension of government, which is only the tip of the social or governance iceberg. It also requires an understanding of the businesses that influence our culture and government. In Washington, the corporations that control the flow of capital and control the Internet exert a significant influence. They also increasingly determine the value and visibility of investments, businesses, and labor, for better or worse. However, they do everything in the dark. It is necessary to develop public options for search and management in order to create environments that are not only transparent but also understandable. If that fails, we can expect a society that is ever more biased in favor of black box insiders and a populace that is ever more ignorant of how its key institutions actually work.

Although we have a limited understanding of how automobile engines work, we are able to sufficiently assess whether they enable us to travel safely and comfortably. We are unable to easily evaluate the performance of the reputation, search, and finance engines. When trade secrecy is in place, it is nearly impossible to determine whether their judgments are legitimate, honest, or fair. There may be illicit motives behind the labeling of a person as a bad job candidate, a website as irrelevant, or a loan as a bad risk; however, in most cases, we will never be privy to the information required to prove that. We do know, however, that those at the top will continue to succeed, largely due to their good name from previous accomplishments; People at the bottom are more likely to face disadvantages that build up. Black box methods are just as likely to enshrine a digital aristocracy as they are to empower experts, despite the 218 THE BLACK BOX SOCIETY promises of freedom and self-determination made by the lords of the information age.

A very different kind of potential exists for open technology applications.

The government could use technology to monitor and control corporate waste and greed on our behalf, rather than using it against American citizens. Our social world would be fairer and easier to understand if technology and governance were available to the public.

Admittedly, demands for dignity, due process, and social justice are contentious; however, rather than conflating ourselves with "an impersonal economy lacking a truly human purpose," we might consider how institutions could be reshaped to meet higher goals than shareholder value98.

There will always be vested privilege holders who would rather not share. Nevertheless, it is time for citizens to demand that significant decisions regarding our financial and communication infrastructures be made immediately comprehensible to independent reviewers and included in a public record that is accessible to all citizens over time.

Our black box society has become dangerously unstable, unfair, and unproductive, despite the fact that black box vices frequently exhibit amazing beauty. Neither the quants of New York nor the engineers of California are capable of establishing a stable society or economy. Those are the responsibilities of a citizenry, which can only carry out its duties effectively if it is aware of the stakes.

Notes AC KNOWLEDGMENTS INDEX NOTES Book Epigraphs Heracleitus, "On the Universe," in Hippocrates IV, Loeb Classical Library 150, translated Jones, W. H. S. (Cambridge: In 1931, Harvard University Press), 501.

"That Nature is a Heraclitean Fire and of the Comfort of the Resurrection," by Gerald Manley Hopkins. Foundation for Poetry. The poem can be found at http://www.poetryfoundation. org/poem/173662.

1 Introduction: What You Need to Know Politics: Harold D. Lasswell Who, When, and How Gets What (New York:

1972, Meridian Books).

2. The Winner-Take-All Society, by Robert H. Frank and Philip J. Cook (New York: 1996 Penguin); The Achieving Society, David C. McClelland, Eastford, CT: 2010; Martino Fine Books Mark Tovey and Hassan Masum, editors,

Cambridge, MA: The Reputation Society 2012; (MIT Press); The Interest Group Society, by Jeffrey M. Berry and Clyde Wilcox (Upper Saddle River, NJ: 2008 Pearson); Robert N. Bellah and others, New York: The Good Society 1992 Vintage);

The Decent Society, Avishai Margalit (Cambridge: 1996 (Harvard University Press). Social order criticism can also take this form; Sick Societies, by Robert B. Edgerton (New York: 1992 (Free Press).

3. Gillian Tett has spoken of the economy's "social silences."

Fool's Gold, Gillian Tett, New York: 2009 (Free Press). Building on Antonio Gramsci's theories, sociologist John Gaventa has focused on what is kept off political agendas as a "third dimension" of power.

Power and Powerlessness, John Gaventa (Champaign: 1982, University of Illinois Press "Deep Secrecy," by David E. Pozen, Stanford Law Review 62 (2010), pp. 257–340.

"Agnotology:" by Robert N. Proctor In Agnotology: A Missing Term to Describe the Cultural Production of Ignorance and Its Study, Ignorance's Making and Breaking, edited by Londa N. Schiebinger and Robert N. Proctor (Stanford, CA: 2008, Stanford University Press),

5. Financial Times, March 29, 2011, "Dodd-Frank Fails to Meet Test of Our Times," by Alan Greenspan; American Economics Review 35, Friedrich A. Hayek, "The Use of Knowledge in Society," 1945: 519– 530. Naturally, according to Richard Bronk, "Hayek's analysis falls short by ignoring the role of dominant narratives, analytical monocultures, self-reinforcing emotions, feedback loops, information asymmetries, and market power in distorting the wisdom of prices." "Hayek on the

Wisdom of Prices:" by Richard Bronk A Reconsideration," *Erasmus Journal of Philosophy and Economics*, vol. 1 (2013): 82– 107.

6. The Nation, November 19, 2003, "The Invisible Hand of Business in the 2012 Election," Lee H. Fang, http://www.thenation.com/arti cle /177252 /invisible -hand -business -2012-election.

7. The term is also polysemic in philosophy. For instance, a given process can be a very useful black box if enough

people simply accept its results as valid. Some aspects of the real world are taken for granted without further investigation. Graham Harman said, "When a statement is simply presented as raw fact without any reference to its genesis or even its author, we have a true black box." Latour asks, "Who used Lavoisier's paper to write the water formula H_2O?" Prince of Networks, Harman: Metaphysics and Bruno Latour (Melbourne: 37). re.press, 2009. This book aims to prevent leading Internet and finance firms from developing into this kind of black box by raising enough questions about their results.

8. Minnesota Law Review 93, Jack Balkin, "The Constitution in the National Surveillance State" (2008): 1– 25.

9. The New Yorker, February 12, 2014, "Amazon and the Perils of Non-Disclosure," by George Packer.

10. "Internet of Things and Ubiquitous Sensing," by Arkady Zaslavsky (September 2013).
Now, computing. It can be

found   at http://www.computer.org/portal/web/ computingnow/archive/september2013.

11. Financial Times, June 10, 2011, "Invasion of the Body Hackers" by April Dembosky

12. "Transparent Predictions" by Tal Zarsky, Illinois Law Review (2013):

1503– 1570.

13. "Wall Street Aristocracy Got $1.2 Trillion in Secret Loans," Bradley Keoun and Phil Kuntz, Bloomberg News, August

22, 2011, http://www.bloomberg.com /news /2011 -08-21 /wall - street aristocracy -got -1 - trillion in -fed -s -secret - loans.html

14. "Financial Sector Back to Accounting for Nearly One-Third of U.S. Profi ts," Maxwell Strachan, Huffington Post (blog), March 30, 2011, http://www.huffingtonpost.co m/2011/03/30 /financial-profi ts-percentage_n_841716.html. In the boom years, things were even better for the finance firms.

15. Who Is in Charge of the Future, Jaron Lanier New York, NY 2013) (Simon & Schuster). The photography company Kodak was worth $28 billion and employed more than 140,000 people at its height of power. NOTES TO PAGES 6–10 223 Even the first digital camera was created by them. However, Instagram has emerged as the new face of digital photography, and Kodak is currently insolvent. Instagram had only thirteen employees when it was sold to Facebook in

2012 for a billion dollars. Ibid., 2.

16. California Law Review 100 (2012), "Information Lost and Found," by Frederic Bloom: 635– 690.

17. Complexity is a byproduct of obfuscation, which is sometimes a byproduct of modern business, but it is also frequently created for ill-gotten gain.

"Why Is Finance So Complex?" by Steve Randy Waldman http://www.interfl uidity.com/v2/2669.html,

Interfl uidity (blog), December 26, 2011.

18. The irremediably unknown is a mystery, according to G.K. Chesterton.

We can't solve or dissect it; rather, we just become more aware of it.

19. This is an established legal issue. See "Circular Priority Systems" by Grant Gilmore, Yale Law Journal 71 (1961): 53–74.

20. The book "What's Inside America's Banks?," by Jesse Eisinger and Frank Partnoy,

January 2, 2013, The Atlantic

21. Ibid.

22. 23. Clay Shirky, "A Speculative Post on the Idea of Algorithmic Authority," Shirky (blog), November 13, 2009, http://www.shirky.com/weblog/2009/11/a -speculative -post -on-the-idea-of-algorithmic-authority/. See The Quants: Scott Patterson's book. How a New Generation of Mathematicians Ruled Wall Street and Nearly Killed It (New York: (2010) (Crown Publishing).

24. The Payoff, Jeff Connaughton: The Reason Why Wall Street Always Wins 2013, Prospecta Press). The title of the book by Connaughton, "The Blob," refers to the covert exchange of favors between government, lobbyists, businesses, media interests, and others. See Hanna Fenichel Pitkin's Attack of the Blob: A Theory and Critical Analysis of the Intermixture of Political and Economic Elites. The Social Concept of Hannah Arendt (Chicago: (2000), University of Chicago Press, p. 5; Wedel,

Janine R., Shadow Elite: Democracy, government, and the free market are undermined by the world's new power brokers (New York: 2009 (Basic Books).

25. Local Justice: Jon Elster How Institutions Divide Necessary and Scarce Assets (New York: 1993 (Russell Sage Foundation)

26. See Risk Savvy: An Insightful Account of Modeling as Rationalization by Gerd Gigerenzer. Good Decision

Making (New York: 2014 (Viking).

27. Bad Pharma, Ben Goldacre: How Pharmaceutical Companies Deceive Doctors and Hurt Patients (London: Third Estate, 2012), p. 3; "Grand Bargains for Big Data:" by Frank Pasquale Maryland Law Review 72, "The Emerging Law of Health Care Information," (2013): 668–772 (collecting studies on health confidentiality).

28. See, for instance, David Dayen's report, "Massive new

fraud coverup: "How banks are pillaging homes — while the government watches," published in Salon on April 23, 2014, at http://www.salon.com/2014/04/23/massive_new_fraud_coverup_how_banks_are_pillaging_homes_while_the_government_watches/; The Private Equity Limited Partnership Agreement Release: Yves Smith, Naked Capitalism published "The Industry's Snowden Moment" on May 28, 2014, at http://www.nakedcapitalism.com/2014/05/private-equity-

limited-partnership-agreement-
release-industrys-snowden-
moment.html.

29. "An Interactive Map of the
Dark-Money Universe," by Dave
Gilson, Gavin Aronsen,
Tasneem Raja, Ben Breedlove,
and E. J. Fox (June 2012). The
Mother Jones Available at the
following URL:
http://www.motherjones.com/
politics/2012/06/interactive-
chart-super-pac-election-
money; "Transparent Elections
After Citizens United," by Ciara
Torres-Spelliscy (Mar. 2011).
New York University School of

Law's Brennan Center for Justice. The document can be found at https://www.brennancenter.org/publication/transparent-elections-after-citizens-united.

Health insurers "publicly stake[d] out a pro-reform position while privately funding the leading antireform lobbying group in Washington" during the Affordable Care Act debate. Izadi, Elahe, "Exclusive: AHIP Gave More Than $100 Million to Chamber's Efforts to Derail Health Care Reform," National Journal (blog), June 13, 2012,

http://www.nationaljournal.co
m/blogs/influencealley/2012/0
6/exclusive AHIP Gave More
Than $100 Million to Chamber's
Efforts to Derail Health Care
Reform

30. Eric Schmidt: Shane
Richmond The Telegraph,
October 5, 2010, "Google Gets
Close to the "Creepy Line""

31. Muckrakers and reformers
like Brandeis were made
possible by publications like
McClure's. "What the Fluck?"
by Adam Curtis
http://www.bbc.co.uk/blogs/ad

amcurtis/posts/WHAT-THE-FLUCK, BBC Blog, December 5, 2013. Curtis also makes the point that today's scandals necessitate such disclosure and explanation, noting that scandals "range from the NSA [U.S. National Security Agency] and GCHQ [Britain's Government Communications Headquarters], to global banks, private equity... and a few components of the media-industrial complex. However, the scandals do not combine to form a larger picture. In addition, our responses can be baffling and contradictory at times, as is the case with surveillance and transparency. It's as if the scandals are pieces of a huge jigsaw puzzle; all we need is for someone to put those pieces together to give us a clear picture of what's going on. Ibid.

32. The Search for Order, Robert H. Wiebe: 1922 (New York: 132) (Farrar, Straus & Giroux, 1967). They knew enough about their lives to know that the old ways and old values wouldn't work anymore.

33. See "The History of Undisclosed Spending in U.S. Elections and How 2012 Became the Dark Money Election" by Trevor Potter and Bryson B. Morgan, Notre Dame Journal of Law, Ethics, and Public Policy 27 (2013):

383– 480.

Printed in Great Britain
by Amazon

17502618R00071